FAUKNER'S WORK

MATT FAUKNER

Copyright © Matt Faukner
All Rights Reserved.

This book has been published with all efforts taken to make the material error-free after the consent of the author. However, the author and the publisher do not assume and hereby disclaim any liability to any party for any loss, damage, or disruption caused by errors or omissions, whether such errors or omissions result from negligence, accident, or any other cause.

While every effort has been made to avoid any mistake or omission, this publication is being sold on the condition and understanding that neither the author nor the publishers or printers would be liable in any manner to any person by reason of any mistake or omission in this publication or for any action taken or omitted to be taken or advice rendered or accepted on the basis of this work. For any defect in printing or binding the publishers will be liable only to replace the defective copy by another copy of this work then available.

To myself

Contents

Foreword

fantastic for a debut book

-writer's network

1. Why not?

why, why should I
waste my time
being stupid and
writing these rhymes
when I can be with you
laying on sand 'n'
looking at your eyes
this deep pair of blue
why, why shouldn't I
give it a try
abandon my lies
and these lone cries
why, why shouldn't I
be by your side
be with you
through 'nd through

2. A rotten kiss

your rotten heart,
made me fall in love.
how was I supposed to know,
your kindness was a mere glove?
your smile on my face
turned into a laugh behind my back,
hurting me became a race
who'd be the first to attack?
the one I fell in love with
or of whom I'm scared?
but it seems like
you came unprepared,
so let's fight.
'nd when we do,
without any mercy i'll
kiss you.

3. Criminal

even if loving you is a crime,
I'll do it every time.
I'll fulfil my sentence willingly,
'nd come back once I'm free.
even if I have to pay a fine,
I'll spend on you my every dime
I'll do everything that has to be done
to make you 'n' me one

4. Unfair love

working too hard,
hoping too much
just for your voice,
or just your touch
knowing it'll never happen
knowing we'll never be one
but can you blame me,
for trying so hard?
you made me fall in love,
'nd chose a different path.
you said it won't work,
you said it won't last.
'nd while I'm stuck here,
you moved on too fast
so how long will it be this way?
it has to end someday
so goodbye 'nd take care
the way you played wasn't fair

5. Stupid smiles

i catch myself smiling stupidly
while looking at you in the polaroid
as I start feeling a little melancholy
i flip the pages to fill the chested void
as i sit on the floor in a daze
i listen carefully to what my mind says,
"whatever your heart hides,
stands crystal clear in your eyes.
you sit 'nd wonder how time flies
you wonder how pain comes in disguise
you sat there 'nd no-one heard your cries,
'nd trust me no one will,
despite your never ending tries."

6. Gasoline

no, you never really loved me,
took it for granted.
now that it's done for,
you so desperately want it.
you kissed me just to shut me up,
told me it was your bloody love.
ah yes it was fatal,
yet i was faithful
take care cuz I'm gonna leave.
not giving a shit about how you feel.
had you told me before,
we wouldn't have gone down this road.

7. Magic

it was magic, yes,
but that of a witch.
'nd indeed i was blessed,
but this time by a bitch
it was magic, yes,
but my happiness couldn't be seen by you.
so you turned it into a mess,
what we had 'n' my mind too.
it was magic, yes,
but look how you messed up
treated it like a game of chess
'nd now your king is outta luck.

8. Addict

never took in any cocaine
never did marjuana
never tried heroin
hell, never sipped vodka
but one can be forgiven if he'd say
I look like an addict all the way
I do look like one, so why not
it does look like I take a daily pot
I have my own beer
my very own liquor
my very taste of a hit
love, sex, music, you name it
they call my home a fantasy land,
it's nothing but a castle built on sand
watch me going to parties every day
blinded by the sun but cant see the grey
they see me with filters 'nd call my life grand
but I take a different woman every night hand in hand
what is love, I cant remember
so tonight I'll try finding it in a pair of eyes made of amber

9. Pushed you away

despite the heavy tears that fell,
i still cannot ask for your help.
there isn't any other way,
I'll have to do it by myself
I pushed you away,
I don't deny.
but all I wanna say is
I didn't want you to cry
sometimes we push away the people we love
those who to us are a gem
we push them to a point of no return
all because we wanna protect them
so my love, understand when say,
that together
we cannot stay
it's either you or me,
one will have to leave

10. A forced smile

'mature beyond her age',
i never doubted.
only if I knew her journey and how she fought it.
she was nicknamed 'therapist of the group'
the one you'd go to, to dry away your tears.
but what if one day she needs a shoulder?
where would she go to ease her fears?
so I sit and wonder
about the reason behind her powers
I see how she took her hurt
'nd out of them built a tower.
she covers her bruises
but all they do is hide
how bad it hurts
in the inside.